the Laurie Berkner

songbook

All songs by Laurie Berkner/Laurissa Anne Berkner BMI
except "O Susannah" (Traditional)
Music arranged for piano, vocal & guitar by David Pearl
Project editor: Heather Ramage
Design: Susan Panetta
Illustrations: Henry Cole
CD recorded, mixed & mastered by Felipe Orozco
Guitar/Bass: David Bradley
Piano: Heather Ramage

This book Copyright © 2007 by Amsco Publications,
A Division of Music Sales Publications, New York.

Order No. AM988383
ISBN-10: 0.8256.3544.6
ISBN-13: 978.0.8256.3544.1

Exclusive Distributors:
Music Sales Corporation
257 Park Avenue South, New York, NY 10010, USA
Music Sales Limited
14-15 Berners Street, London, W1T 3LJ, England
Music Sales Pty. Limited
120 Rothschild Street, Rosebery, Sydney, NSW 2018, Australia

Printed in the United States of America by
Vicks Lithograph and Printing Corporation

Amsco Publications
A Part of The Music Sales Group
New York/London/Paris/Sydney/Copenhagen/Berlin/Tokyo/Madrid

Dear Educators and Parents,

When I started working with pre-schoolers as a music specialist, I had almost no experience with that age group, and I have to say, I wasn't very good at my job! I struggled to connect with the children and felt as though I was relearning a language that I had long forgotten. After weeks of crying at the end of the school day, I finally spoke with the woman who had been my predecessor and asked for her advice. I remember her essentially saying, "Once you start communicating through your music instead of telling the kids what to do, you'll be fine." This piece of advice has influenced much of my writing since and has certainly changed my attitude toward teaching.

Communicating to a child through music is a very personal thing. While this songbook offers ideas and suggestions to enhance the musical experience, remember that the most important place to start from is you, the person sharing the songs, and all the individual feelings and creativity that you bring.

It's also helpful to become conscious of the natural rhythms we all have. Children are especially tuned in to their need to move and then rest, or to explore/move away and then come back to check in with Mom or Dad. To me, this is just like the in and out of breathing, the beating of our hearts, and our cycles of sleeping and waking. I often think about these rhythms when I'm choosing what song to sing next with a group of kids (and often within a song itself, like in "We Are The Dinosaurs"). As human beings we are all sensitive to this, so I would encourage you to pay attention to these instincts when you are singing. Should we get loud or soft in this part of the song? Is it time to get faster or slower? Would a more upbeat song or a more relaxed song work now? Go with what feels right.

Almost every song in this book lends itself to some kind of movement or acting out of words. It could be as simple as lying down for a lullaby, doing a finger play, or acting out a story or game. I hope you'll encourage your kids to use their bodies as well as their voices when you're making this music together.

The CD included contains backing tracks of the songs featured in the activity section. This is so you can be fully involved in the activities and not have to worry about playing the music. All songs in the book have been specially arranged to be accessible to all players—whether you have been playing for six months or six years. Play the full arrangement, or just pick out the tune and chords. We have also included a chord dictionary on page 8 that has easier versions of selected chords if needed.

I hope you get as much out of discovering music together as I do, and most of all, have fun!

♡ Janise
Barton

Contents

Activities and Play Suggestions

The Songbook

Activities and Play Suggestions

When I taught in a classroom or performed music in people's homes, I structured whatever space I was working in by making a circle of masking tape on the floor. This is what I'm talking about when I refer to the "circle" in the activities below. The circle can be used as a basis for almost any song and is useful for helping the children express the songs physically when you only have a small space, or to keep boundaries when in a larger space. Start and end each session by sitting on the edge of the circle, and don't forget to use the backing CD so you can be free to join in!

TIP: Whenever the children are running around the outside of the circle, I would suggest having them all run in the same, predetermined direction to avoid crashes.

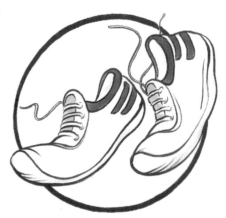

Bumblebee (Buzz Buzz)

TRACK 1

Start with everyone sitting on the circle edge. When you sing the verses, decide how many bees you are singing about, for example, "I saw TWO bumblebees." Then, when you reach "They said their names were..." insert the names of two children in the group. Those chosen go into the middle of the circle to jump and fly about.

When you get to "Oh one, a-two, a-one, two, three, go!" everyone gets up and flies around the outside of the circle, returning to the sitting position (on the circle edge) on the long "Bzzzzzz..." Repeat with different children being chosen to go into the middle.

A good way to end is to bring everyone into the middle at the same time by saying, "I saw lots of bumblebees... They said that they were from [insert name of school, group]."

I'm Gonna Catch You

TRACK 2

Begin the song with everyone running around the outside of the circle. Then have them "jump" into the day of the week by jumping into the middle of the circle—"I jumped into Monday..." They can then act out each activity that happens on the different days.

End by turning around on "Then I turned around..." and have them put a hand up to their ear on "And I heard a sound..." Continue with the running on "I'm gonna catch you..."

At the end when "I'm gonna catch you..." is repeated over and over, chase them around the outside of the circle and try to catch as many of them as you can!

Sneaks

TRACK 3

Have everyone walk around on their tiptoes looking for a "hiding place" during the opening of the song. Look for them and "find" them all during the "When I come out..." part. As you find each one, have them go to the middle of the circle and jump around as, one by one, the others join in.

During the last "La di da" encourage them to run, dance, spin, or move in any way they like, and then to finally flop down in the middle of the circle on their backs until the song is over.

Trucks

TRACK 4

This one is great for acting out the lyrics. Start by sitting around the circle edge and have everyone pretend to put on their "trucker" clothes (hat and pants especially), then scoop up the dirt and sand, just as it says in the song.

On "Drive your truck…" have them "drive" around the outside of the circle. Make the sound of a fire truck siren each time. Continue by acting out the verses, for example, reach up on "You gotta lift it up high…" and reach down on "And bring it down low."

End the song with everyone back around the circle's edge, acting out pulling the truck into the truck stop and filling it with gas. Then do a nice loud "honk" all together to finish!

Here's another idea to encourage them to be creative: before you perform the song, ask the children to make the "shape" of each truck with their bodies. What would a car-carrier look like, or a crane?

Victor Vito

TRACK 5

All percussion works well for this song and is especially good for the younger children. For the older kids, I would encourage them to clap rhythmically throughout and have them try to do a double clap after the words "rice" and "beans" like this:

Sing the third verse quietly and slowly and then have everyone get up and dance, jump, and clap as fast as they can on the last verse.

We Are The Dinosaurs

TRACK 6

Start by marching around the outside of the circle in time with the music. Come to the center and mime eating on "We stop and eat our food…"

March around the outside again on "We are the dinosaurs…" and then come to the center to lie down on "We stop and take a rest…" Pause here and have fun waking them up! March again, and try to save the roaring for the very end so you can build up the excitement.

What Falls In The Fall?

TRACK 7

When I worked as the music specialist at Rockefeller University's Child and Family Center, there was a phenomenal movement teacher named Debra Wanner who taught there at the same time I did. For many years we worked together creating end-of-the-year musical shows in which the children participated. Her wonderfully creative choreography really made it fun for them. My suggestions for this song are based on memories from the late 1990s of what Debra had a classroom of 3-year-olds do when they performed "What Falls In The Fall?" for their parents and teachers. (Anything that doesn't seem to work is surely because my memory is poor and not due to Debra's work!)

1st verse: "Rain falls" Start on tiptoes and have the children wave their fingers like rain falling as they move down toward the floor. Repeat while slowly turning around until the verse is over.

2nd verse: "Temperatures fall" Have the kids hug their bodies and shiver as if they are cold, and then ask them to find someone to hug on "You've got to hug your friends."

Bridge: "And when the leaves start to change" Slow spinning with arms out until "High up in the trees," at which point they reach up as high as they can.

3rd verse: "Leaves fall" Drop down from reaching and continue going up and down, or pretend to rake leaves, until "They twirl everywhere…" where the children twirl. Have them pretend to throw piles of leaves up into the air on "And I throw them in the air…" and finally, everyone stomps around on "They crunch beneath my feet…"

During the instrumental measures, everyone pretends to play in the leaves by throwing them, falling into imaginary piles, kicking them into the air, dancing, running, etc., until the words "Kids fall in the fall…" when they all fall to the ground slowly, "Down, down, down, down, down."

Moon Moon Moon

by Laurie Berkner

Moderately

Moon, moon, moon, shin - ing bright. Moon, moon, moon, my night light.

Hold hands above head, touching thumbs and pointer fingers to make a circle shape. Repeat each time you sing this line.

Open arms out and bring them down to your sides.

Pretend to pull a chain to turn on the light.

(Spoken:) Turn it on. (click) Moon, moon, moon, I can see, moon, moon, moon, you're

Put the sides of your hands up to your eyebrows as if you are trying to look very far away.

tak - ing care of me. Look up, it's the moon. Look up, it's the moon. Look

Pretend to rock a baby.

Point up to the sky with one hand. Continue pointing, alternating hands for the next two phrases.

up, it's the moon up in the sky. It's big and round, and

Slowly raise arms from sides to above your head where hands come together to make a big circle.

I have found that it looks just like a { piz - za } { lem - on } pie.

Open arms out to the side, somewhat above your head, as if you're saying, "Ta-da!"

6

Drive My Car

by Laurie Berkner

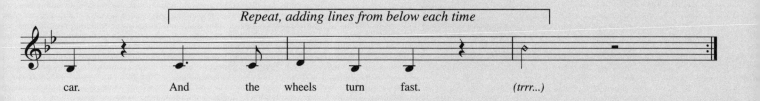

Fast

I'm a-gon-na drive my car, yeah, I'm____ a-gon-na drive my

Repeat, adding lines from below each time

car. And the wheels turn fast. *(trrr...)*

TIP: This works best if you're standing up.

Lyrics

Lyrics	Action
I'm a-gonna drive my car	Hold hands in front of you as if holding a steering wheel, and turn the wheel back and forth.
And the wheels turn fast (trrrr)	Close fists and "roll" them around each other.
And the world goes past (jhoop)	From right to left in front of you, bend the wrist of your right hand up and down making a "wave" with your hand and arm.
And the lights go flash (ch-ch)	Open and close your hands in front of you as if they are "blinking."
And I step on the gas (vroom, vroom)	Pretend to hold the steering wheel and stomp your foot down twice on "vroom, vroom."
And the engine blasts (boom, boom)	Clap once on either side of you for each "boom."
Look out don't crash! (rrrr!)	Make the squeaking sound of brakes, then wipe your forehead and sigh in relief. You made it!
I'm a-gonna park my car	Everyone sits down.

Chord Dictionary

Here are some alternative fingerings for a selection of chords featured in this book.

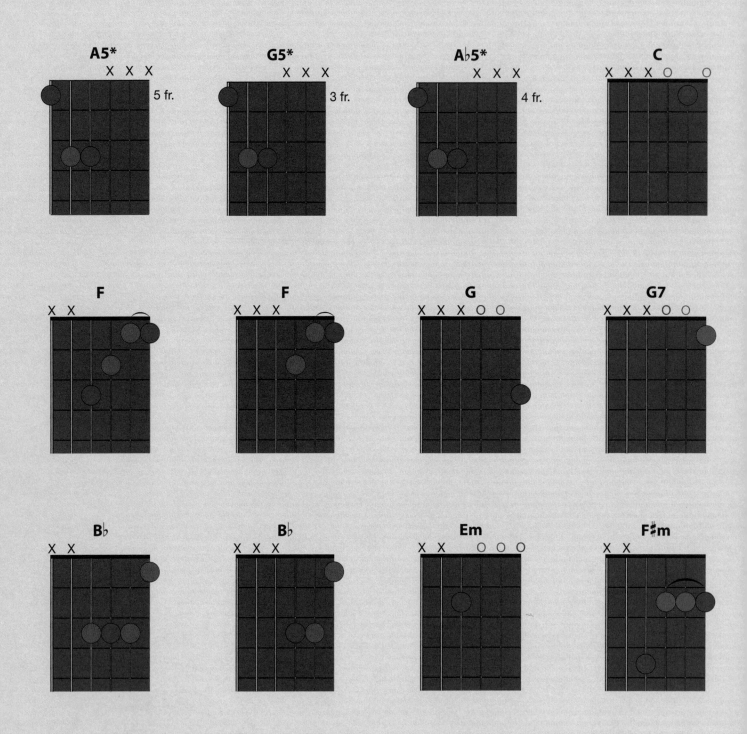

* These "5" chords can be used as a substitute for the A, G and A♭ chords used in "Choc-o-lot In My Pock-o-lot."

I'm Not Perfect

by Laurie Berkner

2. We're not perfect.
No, we're not.
We're not perfect,
But we've got what we've got.
We do our very best, we do our very best.
We do our very best each day.
But we're not perfect
And we hope you like us that way.

3. You're not perfect.
No, you're not.
You're not perfect,
But you've got what you've got.
You do your very best, you do your very best.
You do your very best each day.
But you're not perfect
And you know I love you that way.

Bottle Caps

by Laurie Berkner

Repeat as necessary for Verses 3 & 4

Chorus

1.2.

Chorus

I've got some new ones, old ones, blue ones, gold ones. Ev - 'ry one I see. I've got some red ones, brown ones, flat ones, round ones. Ev - 'ry one I see. Col - lect - ing bot - tle caps, bot - tle caps, bot - tle caps, bot - tle caps, ev - 'ry one I see.

3. I like to pick up rocks.
Big and small ones, too.
I like to pick up rocks.
Some for me and some for you.
I like to pick up rocks,
And bring 'em home with me,
And put my rocks in a box,
And my shells on the shelf,
And keep collecting
(chorus)

4. I like to pick up string.
I find it one, two, three.
I like to pick up string.
Some for you and some for me.
I like to pick up string.
I'll bring it home with me,
And put my string in something,
And my rocks in a box,
And my shells on the shelf,
And keep collecting
(chorus)

Bumblebee (Buzz Buzz)

by Laurie Berkner

2. I was sitting in the pizza place
When I saw two bumblebees.
They said their names were Jackson and Max
And they went...
(chorus)

3. I was flying through the air on a balloon
When I saw three bumblebees (fly past me).
They said their names were Kay and Ray and Fay
And they went...
(chorus)

Choc-O-Lot In My Pock-O-Lot

by Laurie Berkner

2. I wear my shoes and my socks a lot,
And when I paint, I wear a smock a lot,
And when I'm not, what do I got?
Choc-o-lot, I got choc-o-lot,
I got choc-o-lot in my pock-o-lot.

3. Well, the clock, it goes tick-tock a lot,
And I cook my food in a wok a lot,
But when I'm not, what do I got?
Choc-o-lot, I got choc-o-lot,
I got choc-o-lot in my pock-o-lot.

Clean It Up

by Laurie Berkner

Goodnight

by Laurie Berkner

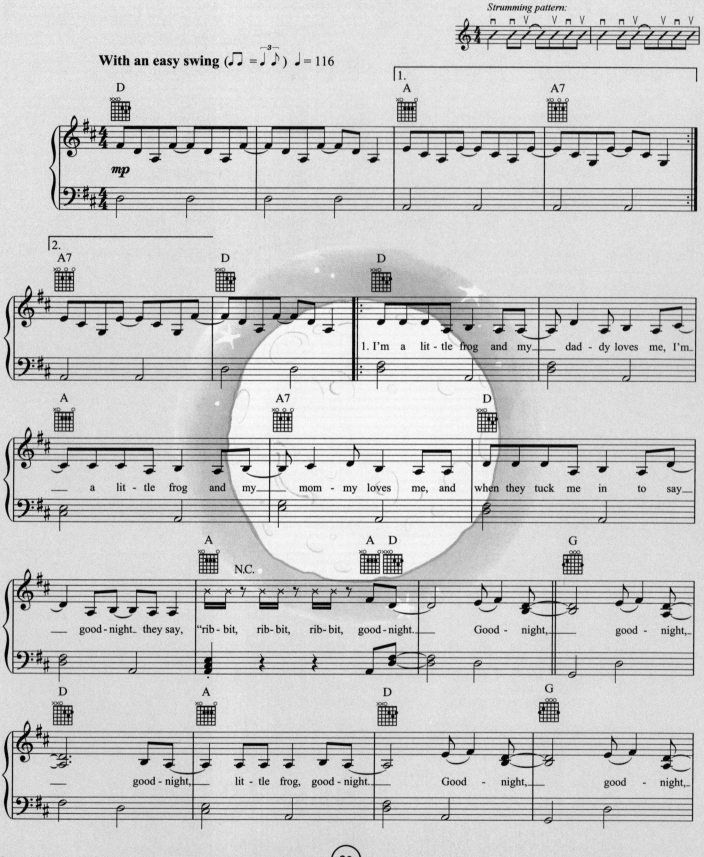

2. I'm a little owl and my daddy loves me,
I'm a little owl and my mommy loves me,
And when they tuck me in to say goodnight
They say, "Hoo, hoo, hoo, goodnight.
Goodnight, goodnight,
Goodnight, little owl, goodnight.
Goodnight, goodnight,
Hoo, hoo, hoo, goodnight."

3. I'm a little tiger and my daddy loves me,
I'm a little tiger and my mommy loves me,
And when they tuck me in to say goodnight
They say, "Rrr, rrr, rrr, goodnight.
Goodnight, goodnight,
Goodnight, little tiger, goodnight.
Goodnight, goodnight,
Rrr, rrr, rrr, goodnight."

4. I'm a little kid and my daddy loves me,
I'm a little kid and my mommy loves me,
And when they tuck me in to say goodnight
They say, "Goodnight, honey, goodnight.
Goodnight, goodnight,
Goodnight, little darlin', goodnight.
Goodnight, goodnight,
Goodnight, goodnight, goodnight."

I Know A Chicken

by Laurie Berkner

2. Shake 'em slow.
   You know how it goes.
   Shake 'em fast.
   Oh, shake those eggs.

3. Can you shake 'em in a circle?
   Oh, 'round and 'round.
   Don't you let 'em touch the ground.
   'Cause you shake 'em 'round and 'round.
   Now shake 'em up and down.
   Oh, shake 'em up and down.
   Shake those eggs.

I Really Love To Dance

by Laurie Berkner

2. My mom said, "Walk backwards."
I gave it a try.
My friends all walk backwards
And sometimes so do I.
But the only thing I really want to do is dance.
(chorus)

3. My mom said, "Try painting."
I painted the sky.
My friends all like painting
And sometimes so do I.
But the only thing I really want to do is dance.
(chorus)

I'm Gonna Catch You

by Laurie Berkner

accel. poco a poco

(G) heard a sound.
(G7) It said,
(G7) It said, I'm gon-na catch you,
(C) (F) you'd bet-ter run. (C) (F) I'm gon-na catch you, (C) here I come. (C) here I come. I caught you!

2. I'm gonna catch you, you'd better run.
I'm gonna catch you, here I come.
So I jumped into Tuesday,
Had myself a snooze day.
Then I turned around
And I heard a sound.
It said...

3. I'm gonna catch you, you'd better run.
I'm gonna catch you, here I come.
So I jumped into Wednesday,
Had a make-new-friends day.
But then I turned around
And I heard a sound.
It said...

4. I'm gonna catch you, you'd better run.
I'm gonna catch you, here I come.
So I jumped into Thursday,
Had myself a nurse day.
But then I turned around
And I heard a sound.
It said...

5. I'm gonna catch you, you'd better run.
I'm gonna catch you, here I come.
And I jumped into Friday,
Had myself a shy day.
But then I turned around
And I heard a sound.
It said...

6. I'm gonna catch you, you'd better run.
I'm gonna catch you, here I come.
So I jumped into Saturday,
And I had a baseball batter day.
But then I turned around
And I heard a sound.
It said...

7. I'm gonna catch you, you'd better run.
I'm gonna catch you, here I come.
So I jumped into Sunday,
I had a super-fun day.
But then I turned around
And I heard a sound.
It said...
I'm gonna catch you *(etc.)*

Mahalo

by Laurie Berkner

28

2. Mahalo for the air I breathe.
Mahalo for my dad and my mom.
My sisters and my brothers and my good friends.
Mahalo for sharing my song.
(chorus)

3. *(Instrumental solo)*
(chorus)

My Energy

by Laurie Berkner

1.2. A7

I have en - er - gy____ Oh, this is

3. A7

I have en - er - gy____ Oh, this is

Coda

D

And it's the

A

on - ly thing that I can be.

D

Yeah, I'm the

Strumming pattern:

A

on - ly thing that I can

D

be.

D

Me,

C   D

me, en - er - gy.

C   D

Me, me, en - er - gy.

C   D

Me, me, en - er - gy,

C   D

Me, me, me.

2. I'm gonna wave my arms.
I'm gonna shake my hips.
I'm gonna jump to the sky.
Because I have energy.
(chorus)

3. I'm gonna clap my hands.
I'm gonna shake my head.
I'm gonna yell out loud.
Because I have energy.
(chorus)

O Susannah

Traditional

2. It rained all night the day I left,
The weather it was dry.
The sun so hot I froze to death,
Susannah, don't you cry.
(chorus)

3. *Instrumental solo*
(chorus)

4. Well, I had a dream the other night
When everything was still.
I dreamed I saw Susannah
Comin' down the hill.

5. A buckwheat cake was in her mouth
And a tear was in her eye.
Says I, "I'm comin' from the South!"
Susannah, don't you cry.
(chorus)

Pig On Her Head

by Laurie Berkner

Strumming pattern:

Fast ♩ = 192

E B7 E

1. Lau-rie's got a pig on her head. Lau-rie's got a pig on her head.

A B7

Lau-rie's got a pig on her head. She keeps it there all

E

day. 2. My

E B7 E

dad has got a cow on his head. My dad has got a cow

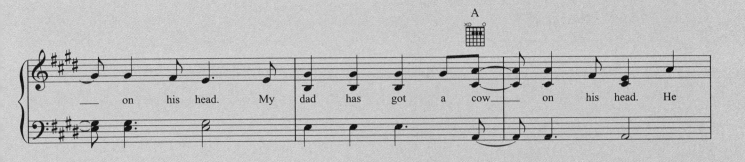

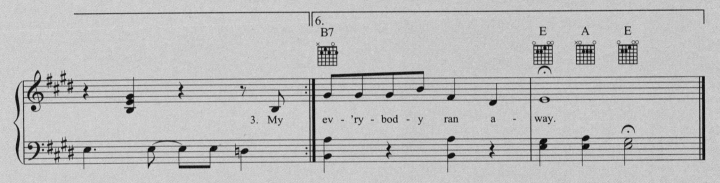

3. My mom has got a sheep on her head.
My mom has got a sheep on her head.
My mom has got a sheep on her head.
She keeps it there all day.

4. My sister's got an alligator on her head.
My sister's got an alligator on her head.
My sister's got an alligator on her head.
She keeps it there all day.

5. My brother's got an elephant on his head.
My brother's got an elephant on his head.
My brother's got an elephant on his head.
He keeps it there all day.

6. My cousin's got his hair on his head.
My cousin's got his hair on his head.
My cousin's got his hair on his head.
He keeps it there all day.

7. And my dog has got a skunk on his head.
My dog has got a skunk on his head.
My dog has got a skunk on his head.
And everybody ran away.

Rocketship Run

by Laurie Berkner

2. Take me to the moon.
Take me to the moon.
When I get there I'll go dancing through the air,
Dancing on the moon.
(chorus)

3. Take me to the stars.
Take me to the stars.
When I get there I'll go jumping through the air,
Jumping from star to star.
(chorus)

4. Take me to the earth.
Leave me on the ground.
When I get there I'll be home.
Ten, nine, eight, seven, six, five, four, three, two, one,
Blastoff! Another rocketship run.

Song In My Tummy

by Laurie Berkner

2. I've got a song in my toes and it wants to come out,
I've got a song in my toes.
I've got a song in my toes and it wants to come out,
I've got a song in my toes.
I've got a song in my toes and it wants to come out,
And when it does I'm gonna sing and shout.
La, la, la, la, la, la, la, la, la,
I've got a song in my toes.

3. I've got a song in my nose and it wants to come out...

4. I've got a song in my bones and it wants to come out...

5. I've got a song in my heart and it wants to come out...

39

This Hat

by Laurie Berkner

2. I have a construction hat
It fits me perfectly.
And when I put it on my head
You'll see what I can be.
I'll use my hammer,
I'll use my hacksaw,
Tear down the building,
I'll use a wrecking ball.
(chorus)

3. I have a birthday hat
It fits me perfectly.
And when I put it on my head
You'll sing "Happy Birthday" to me.
'Cause it's my birthday,
Happy birthday,
Yeah, it's my birthday,
Happy, happy birthday.
(chorus)

Trucks

by Laurie Berkner

3. You could be a forklift,
Or a steam roller.
A backhoe,
Or a dump truck.

4. You could be a car-carrier,
Or a cement mixer.
You could drive a crane,
Or a bulldozer.
(chorus)

5. It's time to get a little bit of gas:
You gotta pull your truck into the truck stop,
Pull your truck into the truck stop,
And fill 'er up.
(Blup, blup, blup...)
Honk, honk.

Under A Shady Tree

by Laurie Berkner

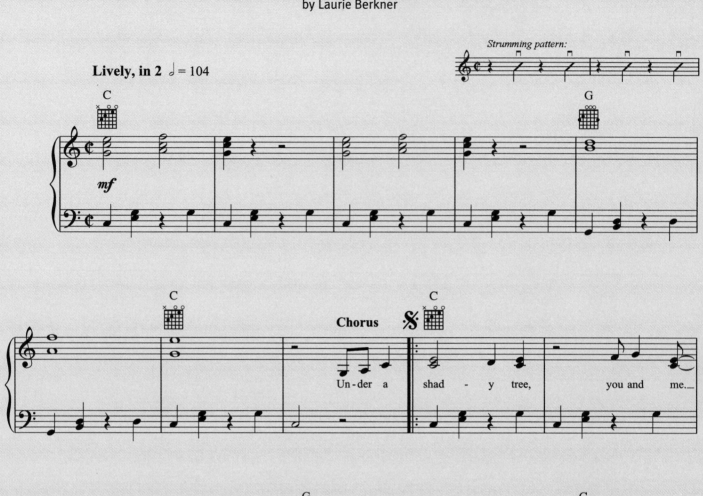

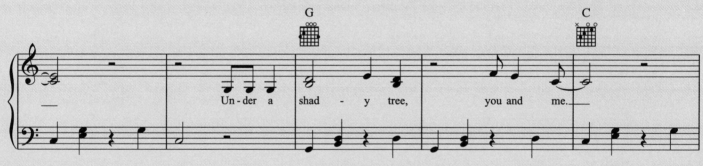

2. Can you feel the soft, cool grass?
Can you feel it with your toes?
We can sit here while it grows.
(chorus)

3. If you want to close your eyes
And sleep beneath the tree
You can rest your head on me.
(chorus)

Victor Vito

by Laurie Berkner

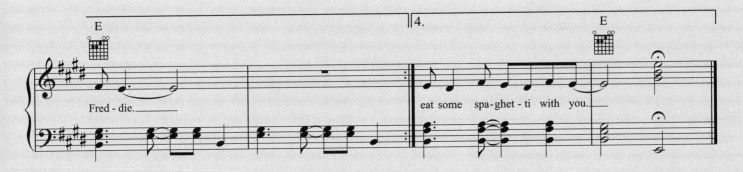

2. Victor Vito and Freddie Vasco
Moved from El Cerrito all the way to Alaska.
Oh, they ate their rice, they ate their beans,
They ate their rutabagas and they ate their collard greens.
(chorus)

3. Victor Vito and Freddie Vasco
They liked to eat slow, they never eat fast.
Oh, they ate their rice, they ate their beans,
They ate their rutabagas and they ate their collard greens.
(chorus)

4. Victor Vito and Freddie Vasco
They liked to eat fast, they never eat slow.
Oh, they ate their rice, they ate their beans,
They ate their rutabagas and they ate their collard greens.
(chorus)

N.B. In the original recording, verse 3 modulates up one half step to F major and then back down to E major for verse 4.
The tempo also slows down for verse 3 and speeds up significantly for verse 4.

Walk Along The River

by Laurie Berkner

2. When I jump along the river,
I jump a step, I jump a step, I jump another step...

And I love to watch the river flow.
I love to watch the river flow.
(chorus)

3. When I dance along the river,
I dance a step, I dance a step, I dance another step...

And I love to watch the river flow.
I love to watch the river flow.
(chorus)

We Are The Dinosaurs

by Laurie Berkner

2. We stop and take a rest
Over in our nest.
We stop and take a rest at the end of the day.
We stop and take a rest
Over in our nest.
We stop and take a rest and then you'll hear us say... that
(chorus)

What Falls In The Fall?

by Laurie Berkner

2. What falls in the fall?
Temperatures fall.
Down, down, down, down, down.
It's when the summer ends,
You've got to hug your friends
To keep your body warm in the fall.

Sneaks

by Laurie Berkner

Strumming pattern: (verse)

Strumming pattern: (chorus)

Moderately ♩ = 96

1. I'm a lit - tle sneak, I hide and seek be - hind the clos - et door.

Verse

I'm a lit - tle sneak, I like to creep a - cross the bath - room floor.

I'm a lit - tle sneak, I'm peek - ing out from un - der - neath the bed.

F　　　　　　　　　　　　　　　　　　G

I'm a lit - tle sneak, I'm hid - ing with the sheets o - ver my head.

Chorus
G

When I come out, it's time to say＿ it: two/three/four sneaks are more＿ fun to play with.

1.2.　　　　　　　　　　　　　　　　　　　3.

And　　　La di da＿

D　　　F　　　C　　　G　　　D

＿ di da,＿＿＿ da.＿ La di da＿ di

2. I'm a little sneak, you'll never know the places that I hide.
I might be behind a tree, but you won't look outside.
I'm a little sneak, I'm small enough to fit into tight spaces.
I'm a little sneak and I know all the sneaky hiding places.
(chorus)